THE
Archive Photographs
SERIES

BURTON
TO
HESWALL

The Middle Slipway, Parkgate.

THE
Archive Photographs
SERIES

BURTON
TO
HESWALL

Compiled by
Pat O'Brien

CHALFORD

First published 1996
Copyright © Pat O'Brien, 1996

The Chalford Publishing Company
St Mary's Mill, Chalford,
Stroud, Gloucestershire, GL6 8NX

ISBN 0 7524 0628 0

Typesetting and origination by
The Chalford Publishing Company
Printed in Great Britain by
Redwood Books, Trowbridge

Brevet-Maj. W. La T. CONGREVE, V.C.

Gallahers Tobacco Co. issued eight series of cigarette cards (twenty five per set) between 1915-18 dedicated to those awarded the Victoria Cross in the war. Major William La Touche Congreve of Burton Hall was one of them.

Contents

This a page from the *Daily Graphic* in October 1892. The bottom illustration shows the Prime Minister, Mr Gladstone, cutting the first sod in a railway line that was built to run down the centre of Wirral and opened in 1896. One of its many titles was the North Wales and Liverpool Railway.

Woodbank Tollgate.

Introduction

Most of the places recorded in this book border on the Dee estuary and so it is not surprising that their past has experienced a strong maritime influence. The lost Roman road from the fortress at *Deva* (Chester) started at the *Porta* (Gate of Ten Men, Northgate) and skirted along inland through the northern fringe on its way to Meols. Many local placenames have their origin in Anglo Saxon and Norse nomenclature. Shotwick was recorded in monastic charters, its royal ford into Wales used by the armies of the Earls of Chester and Edward I. When the River Dee started to silt up in the fifteenth century surveys were carried out to locate safe new anchorages and the port of Chester moved further up the estuary to Lightfotepole near Great Saughall and the New Quays at Ness and Parkgate. It then became necessary to turn ancient trackways and lanes into passable roads and then later into turnpikes.

The earliest public transport services were the stagecoaches between Chester and the ports later to be replaced by omnibuses and the railway. There were two phases to the entry of railways into the Wirral. First in 1866 came the branch line from Hooton to Parkgate, with stations at Hadlow Road, serving Willaston and Neston. This line was later extended to West Kirby in 1886 with stations at Heswall, Thurstaston and others. The second railway line (see p. 6) brought stations to Burton Point (1899), Neston and Heswall Hills (1898) and Barnston.

This area of Wirral has seen a remarkable number of its sons win high military honours in times of war and many of these titles are illustrated here.

Many of the photographs that have been used here are the work of professional photographers of Wirral's past. Those that are known or can be identified include Mr A. Maycock and Mr V. Crook of Parkgate, Mr Bevan and Mr H. Middleton Jones of Heswall and Mr E.R. Jones and Mr George Davies of Port Sunlight. Much is owed also to amateur photographers whose pictures appear here and particularly, for example, the railway enthusiast who had the foresight to record the closing years of the Hooton to West Kirby line which is now The Wirral Way. There are some photographers that I have failed to trace, to these my thanks and apologies.

I hope you will enjoy this record of a small part of your local heritage and, if you have a camera, why not think about recording some of your still changing environment yourself for the benefit of future generations and their local historians!

Pat O'Brien
Ellesmere Port
February 1996

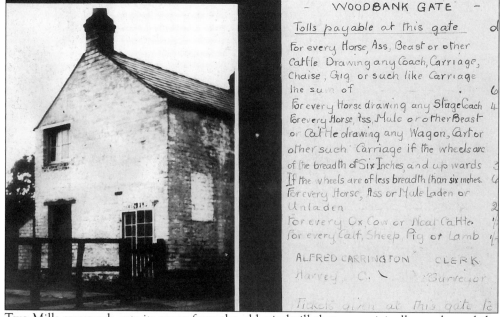

Two Mills crossroads gets its name from the old windmill that was originally nearby and the new windmill built in 1777 at Great Saughall. The cafe in the background was always a favourite stop for cyclists. This is the original building in 1907.

One
Around Burton

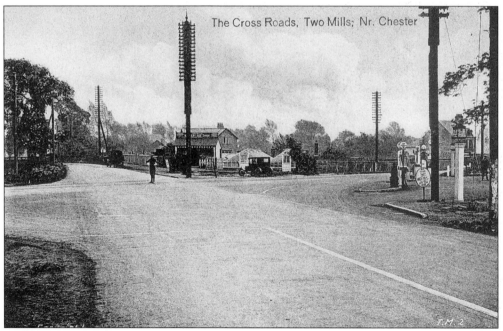

The Cross Roads, Two Mills; Nr. Chester

Two Mills crossroads in the 1930s shows a new cafe building and a garage on the opposite corner. The road past the cafe leads down to Queensferry, the way to Wales.

A small cottage cafe has become this large building by 1912. It is now called 'Claremont' and serves lunches and high teas under the management of Wm. Pepper.

Lower Ferry at Queens Ferry (originally known as Kings Ferry) handled a lot of horse-drawn vehicles. In the background can be seen the road bridge nearing completion which was about to replace it.

This is an ancient road that led over the sands and channels of the Dee estuary into Wales. It is recorded that Henry III in 1245 and also Edward I in 1278 led their armies this way. It was marked on ancient maps that because of tidal changes a local guide was recommended.

At one time the last house on the left was an ancient inn called the Black Greyhound. In the seventeenth century the curate of Shotwick performed several irregular marriages here. Those involved were found out and appeared before the Bishop's Court at Chester.

Inside the churchyard gate is the village war memorial erected after the First World War. A new inscription relating to the Second World War includes the name: Frederick Hopwood, killed at the Battle of Arnhem, 17 September 1944.

This photograph was taken by a German war photographer and shows the battlefield grave of the above named Frederick Hopwood. The photograph appeared in *Berliner Illustrierte Zeitung* No. 44, 2 November 1944.

The interior of the church has hardly changed since this postcard view was taken in 1910.

Shotwick Hall was built in 1622 by Joseph Hockenhull of Hockenhull and Shotwick. The family lived mainly at Hockenhull near Tarvin and their second son lived in this house. Their coat of arms is a curious one - an asses head.

Puddington village has outwardly changed little over the years. Called *Potitone* in the Domesday Book, the manor was held for seven centuries by the Massey family who lived at Puddington Hall.

In 1875 when the Cop was made at Burton Point a large number of giant skeletons were found, some buried in wicker or straw coffins. Tradition says that they were Irish Catholic labourers that were drowned in a storm and so not buried in a churchyard.

Rose Cottage at Burton Point.

Although this railway line was built and opened in 1896 (see p. 6) Burton Point did not have a station until 1 August 1899. The line still has a passenger service but the station closed in 1955. This photograph was taken in 1961.

Looking back towards Puddington. Beyond the trees on the left is White House Farm. This postcard was posted 28 August 1908.

A scene in the early 1900s looking down the High Street. The people in the picture are passing Elm Tree Farm on the left.

The church tower has a single finger clock. Calibration marks between the hours are quarters. In the days before buses and trains seven and a half minutes either way was not so important!

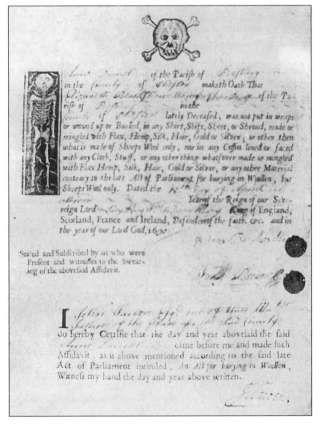

Burial Woolen Afadavits were handed in at funerals to be entered into parish records in compliance with the Burial Woolen Act of 1667.

The inscription on the grave reads: 'The body of Elk… 1663 the word has been'. The quarker community referred to is believed to have been associated with a farm of the name Elkthorns (or Hellthorns) near Denhall Lane c. 1890.

The Quakers Graves, Burton.

When the Gladstone family owned the estate sections of the wood were fenced off and rights of way were blocked. It was done to preserve the game but it led to disputes with the local people.

ROAD THROUGH THE WOODS, BURTON.

"The Unique

In parish registers John Haggasman, miller to the Masseys at Burton, is recorded as having been killed by a thunderbolt in October 1579 and Edward Sumner, miller at Burton, to have died suddenly in March 1629. Mill records for this site go back to 1298 and this was the second peg mill here.

The mill was rebuilt by Sir W. Massey in 1629 and finally ruined by a great gale in 1882.

The main source of water for the village came from Hampston's Well in Station Road. Those people unable to fetch their own supply could buy it from this watercart for tuppence a bucket (J. Ryan colln.).

The building on the left is the wheelwright's shop, also the site of the original smithy. The second smithy can be seen further up the road on the left. In 1878 the wheelwright was Joseph Jones and the blacksmith was Robert Venables (J. Ryan colln.).

The cottages on the hill overlooking the blacksmith's shop, 1890-2.

A scene at the Burton smithy. In 1869 there were two blacksmiths at Burton; John Edwards and Robert Venables. Ness had Samuel Mealor and Neston had Samuel Anyon, Robert Evans and Mark Flood.

Walter Norris Congreve (right) was born at Congreve, Staffordshire in 1862. He won the Victoria Cross 15 December 1899 in the South Africa War attempting to save the guns at Colenso. In this formal study he is standing with his son Christopher John, both of them in dress uniform of the Rifle Brigade. His other son is featured on the opposite page. When Walter's father Captain Congreve died in January 1902 at Burton Manor he inherited the estate. He later became a Lieutenant General and was knighted.

William Le Touche Congreve was born at Burton Hall 22 March 1891. He was killed 20 July 1916 to the north of Delville Wood at the age of twenty five years. He was awarded the Victoria Cross for conspicuous acts of bravery between July 5 and 20. When he was killed his father, then a Lieutenant General, was nearby at a Fourth Army Conference and afterwards visited the body of his son and kissed him goodbye. He was the first officer in the Great War to be awarded the VC, the DSO and the MC.

From 1805 until 2 February 1903 Burton Hall was the home of the Congreve family. When sold to Henry Neville Gladstone it became Burton Manor. The building was considerably altered and a lot of changes took place throughout the estate. This view is from 1906.

Henry Neville Gladstone was born in 1852 the third son and the sixth child of W.H. Gladstone the great Liberal Prime Minister. He was married in 1889 to Maud Ernestine Rendell the daughter of a close friend of his father. They had no children and were at Burton Manor for nineteen years.

This building is known as Sunny Bank Cottage. The hand made bricks used in its construction suggest that it is of a great age.

The village shop in 1906. The sign says, 'Ale'. In the 1906 local directory Marley Murtagh is listed as shopkeeper.

Barn End before the First World War. This cottage was formerly the inn known as Fishermans Arms, later Noahs Ark.

Now known as Stanley House this was once the Stanley Arms one of the two village inns. It got its name from the Stanley family who opened the first colliery at Ness.

This road leads on to Ness. The first house on the left is the old post office (see below) and the house on the right is the White House Farm.

This image comes from a postcard posted at Chester General Railway Station 28 April 1905 shows Burton post office. Over the door the inscription reads, M. Cottrell, Licensed to sell Tobacco.

Rake Cottage is believed to have been a seventeenth-century cottage with a timber-frame and exterior of handmade bricks. It is situated between Rake House and Manor Villas.

This cottage was the home of Nurse Jones who served the communities of Two Mills, Ledsham and Puddington as well as Burton between 1924 and 1950.

Bishop Wilson was born here in 1663 and was for fifty eight years Bishop of Sodor and Man. When he died he was buried in an elm coffin which came from a tree he had planted as a young man.

Burton School was founded by Bishop Wilson in 1724 to provide free education for the children of Burton Parish. This photograph was taken in the early 1900s.

William Lawton was a locally famous wildfowler who built his own house on the Old Quay. Local people called it Lawton's Quay. He also built punts for wildfowlers.

Although the old Harp Inn was built for the colliery miners it was also very handy for the wildfowlers returning from a shoot on the marshes.

Wildfowlers of the Dee in 1890; L.N. Brookes, J.A. Dockray and Ned Kenny. John Dockray was for a time the engineer in charge of the extension of the railway from Parkgate to West Kirby. In 1897 L.N. Brookes, a widower, moved to Gayton and took his gunpunt with him resuming his hunting from there.

Ness Colliery Farm account, from September the 28th 1776 ending December the 23 1776

The first mine workings were called Ness Colliery Farm and were situated at Denhall and owned by the Stanley Massey family. These are their accounts for 1776. As their workings extended under other peoples lands they paid a proportion of the coal to them.

In 1790 the Stanleys had a pit navigation (underground canal) built under the Dee estuary, known as No. 6 Pit Navigation. Not to be outdone Mr Cottingham, a rival colliery owner, built one too and called it No. 10 Pit Navigation.

In 1832 the Cottingham Colliery (later Neston Colliery) was flooded and a number of pit ponies were drowned. The ponies were bred and stabled underground. It is said that the one pony could count the boxes to be hauled in a shift; one more than eight and he would not move!

An ex-miner recalls that once when seeking a new seam to work they were told of an old four feet seam at about sixty feet depth. They began to dig from the cage at that depth but a sudden rush of hundreds of gallons of water from the excavation sent the cage spinning - the seam was worked out and flooded.

This was the last shift. In the picture, left to right, are: A. Jones, D. Parry, J.Burkey, J. Millington, B. Williams, R. Williams, J.M. Williams, J. Campion, H. Williams, J. Jones. Bill William's grandfather came from Llanberis to work at the mine; four of the family are in the photograph. Bill started work at thirteen and a half years old for 5/- per day as a screen worker on the surface.

Mr C. Millington with an explosive drill. Black Damp was a terrible gas, 'there were thousands of mice in that mine and when the gas began to build up, like when miners broke through into a new cavity, they all used to squeal. The noise was deafening and you had to get out'!

The only general store in the village of Ness at one time was situated at the far end of this thatched cottage. In 1869 the shopkeeper was Hugh Roberts.

This was the general stores in Mill Lane, Ness in 1940.

Ness Holt School in 1932. In the picture are, back row: -?-, -?-, A. Smith, J. Price, P. Swanborough, C. Davis, E. Cottrell, E. Robinson, W. Mealor. Second row: E. Robinson, R. Jones, H. Pickton, R.Leighton, ? Davidson, E. Lawton, E. Ostin, D. Norman, P. Leighton. Third row: G. Roberts, G. Norman, V. Smith, E. Wooley, E. Smith (Cissie), E. Withers, M. Smith, A. Lawton, O. Hughes, M. Wellings. Fourth row: J. Herrigan, B. Wellings, E. Cottrell, L. Lewis, J. Jones, P. Candyland. Front row: B. Monigan, ? Jones, E. Gillett, J. Austin, B. Barnes, J. Anyon, A. Leighton.

Ness School, also in 1932, the senior pupils. Back row: L. Lewis, W. Mealor, E. Ostin, J. Ostin, E. Cottrell. Second row: E. Wooley, R. Jones, E. Small (see p. 100), M. Smith, V. Smith. Front row: K. Wellings, J. Kerrigan, B. Barnes, A. Leighton, B. Monaghan. In front: O. Hughes, M. Austin.

Not far away from the cottages of Ness village are the private residences of Ness Holt with their extensive gardens and box hedges.

St Winifred's R.C. church on Burton Road. The photograph was taken in 1906 and the priest standing in front is Revd Father Bernard Thompson.

Shown here in the 1930s is the second Royal Oak to stand facing the Green at Little Neston.

This is Neston Cottage Hospital in Little Neston in 1922.

The large building on the left is the Institute which was demolished in 1928.

Thirty years on, the Green has been smartened up. The group of cottages on the right are called Hope Cottages.

The Council School in Little Neston was opened in 1909 on the Burton Road.

This view looks down Bull Hill. The last building on the right was once the Bull and Dog inn. In 1869 the innkeeper was William Roberts and in 1905 it was Matthew Roberts.

40

Moorside got its name from the marshy ground between it and the estuary. Because it adjoined the old Quay House it is frequently mentioned in archive documents.

This view, taken before the First World War shows an area now covered with housing developments.

The old Quay House as it was in 1941. It was demolished in 1944.

There are records of the Quay House dating from 1541 to 1604, giving the history of the New Haven harbour, the various uses the house has been put to and also accounts of the people who have occupied it.

Two

Neston

Part of a multi-view postcard showing a small motor train in Neston Station on the Bidston line. This station opened in 1896 and the train was operated by a small steam engine in the front section seen here.

In 1732 on the Mostyn Estate map there is one small mill, near the fork in the two roads Leighton and Wood Lane. In the 1814 estate map the earlier mill is shown with the symbol of a circle, and a second mill is shown further from the fork with the mill cottage between the two. The Tythe Map of 1847 shows only one remaining mill, the one furthest from the fork, thus the mill which has gone, was the one built in 1729. This mill was worked until about 1885. There are records of millers since 1672. Those between 1860-1875 included James Jadely, others were Robert Bridson 1887 and Mrs Eliza Radely.

This house is on Bridge Street and the hill leads into Neston. The steam tractor on its own could operate a thresher and in conjunction with another could plough by means of an interconnecting cable across the field.

This Neston Station was opened in 1866 when the line went as far as Parkgate. It was situated at the junction of Mellock Lane and Bushell Road.

Neston Ladies Day in 1870.

This is the Neston Ladies Day in 1911. Here the background is interesting because we have a good view of the old Brown Horse Inn, its upstairs windows providing a bird's eye view of the events.

This road which extends into the one seen in the view below, was originally part of the turnpike which led from Chester to the Port of Parkgate via Neston.

This shop is at the corner of Gladstone Road. Chester Road terminated here and Hinderton Road extended up to the main Chester highway as it still does today.

The Liberal Club was built in 1901-02. At this period the Liberal Party was well supported in Wirral. Later on it became the Neston Institute and is still in use today as the Civic Hall.

A popular venue was the Bowling Green at the back of Neston Institute.

Albert Fleming, builder, had premises in Leighton Road around 1900. The man fourth from the left is William Ashbrook.

A group of local dignitaries listening to a speech by T.L. Dodd Esq. JP at the laying of the foundation stones of the new Wesleyan Church, at Neston on 27 June 1908.

A quite day in Neston High Street.

This is a group from Neston Presbyterian Sunday School departing on their annual excursion in 1910.

Local people gather around Neston Cross to celebrate the Coronation of King George V and Queen Mary 11 May 1911. They are seen here singing the National Anthem.

King George V at Hooton Station in 1914. He was on his way, in the Royal Train, to officially open Port Sunlight Station. Seen here is 1st Neston Boys Brigade. Facing the king is Mr William Covintry and his son Frank is near left, holding the rifle.

Christopher Bushell was born in Neston on October 31 1888. He was named after his grandfather (see page 59). During World War I he became a T/Lieut. Colonel commanding 7th (S) Bn., The Queen's Royal West Surrey Regt. (S.R.). On 23 March 1918 west of St. Quentin's Canal and north of Tergnier, France, Lt.Col. Bushell personally led C Company of his Battalion who were co-operating with an allied regiment in a counter attack. In the course of this attack he was severely wounded in the head, but carried on, walking in front of both English and Allied troops, encouraging them and visiting every portion of the lines in the face of terrific machine gun fire. He refused to go to the rear and had to be removed to the dressing station in a fainting condition. He was Gazetted the Victoria Cross on 3 May 1918 and died on 8 August 1918. He also earned the Distinguished Service Order.

This group photograph was taken in 1922 at the wedding of Mr J.W. Peters who was a grocer in Neston. His mother can be seen in the Campion family group on p. 61.

High Street, Neston in the early 1930s, looking towards the Cross.

This is Park Street in the early 1900s and the furthest building to the right is the Plough Inn. At that time it was one of the oldest in Neston. In 1869 the landlord was William Hughes and in 1914 it was James Gilbert. By 1924 it was no longer registered as an inn and had reverted to a house.

This is Neston Amateur Football Club in the season 1919-20.

A class in Neston Council School in the 1930s.

Throughout the 1920s and the 1930s, there was a number of private schools in the Neston and Parkgate area.

Neston Home Guard. Back row, left to right: Jim Matthews, -?-, Tom Tilston, Ernest Jellicoe, -?-, Charles Seymour, -?-, Roy Cameron, -?-, -?-, ? Leonard, Bill Parry, Ted Gunning. Middle row: Jack Minshell, Steve Scarrett, Walter Main, George Pearson, ? Pierce, George Fairhurst, ? Partridge, Charlie Jellicoe, Laurence Whitter, -?-, Jack Parr, Harry Foot, -?-. Front row: Joe Mealor, -?-, George Bromelow, ? Lee, Frank Hope (in civvies), Ken Montgomery (CO), Bill Jackson, ? Webster, Billy Cottrell, Frankie Dolan, Walter Mosedale. Together, the Neston, Little Neston and Burton platoons comprised 'A' Coy of No.3 Section of the Cheshire Home Guard with H.Q. based at Hinderton Mount. The Neston platoon was in the Town Hall, with look-out posts on the roof of Mostyn House School, in a purpose-built bunker at the Old Quay.

This photograph from Neston Library of a group in a garden in the 1930s is a bit of a mystery! Can anyone identify the event or recognise any of the people?

Neston Co-op Women's Guild in the late 1940s or early 1950s. One lady has been identified as Mrs Regan.

Two scenes from the 1953 Coronation street party held at Park Street.

THE CROSS & PARKGATE RD. NESTON.
COPYRIGHT.

Mavcock, Photo., Parkgate.

In the days when there was not much traffic, the Bushell Fountain was a popular meeting place. It was erected by local citizens in 1882 as a tribute to Christopher Bushell Esq., well-known for his many acts of generosity.

PARKGATE ROAD, NESTON, CHESHIRE.

A closer view of the shops at the Neston end of the Parkgate Road, with shops displaying their wares outside, including the butchers on the left.

Parkgate Road, before the First World War showing Church Lane on the right.

The father of George Gunn VC (see page 85), George Gunn MD had a surgery at Radcliffe on this road. He was also physician, surgeon and anesthetist to the Royal Liverpool County Hospital for Children at Heswall.

Three
Parkgate

This is the second station to have been here and it was built in 1886. There was a subway beneath the line connecting each platform. From here the mineral railway that was connected in 1877 (see introduction) ran down to the Wirral Colliery by the shoreline. (J. Ryan, collection)

Station Road Cottages, with a glimpse of the sea, in the 1900s. The last house on the right, No.16 is reputed to have been the house where Emma Lyon stayed in June 1784, when she came to bathe in the sea water for its health properties.

This is an early view of the buildings that fronted the south end of the promenade.

Capt. G. Collins' 1689 Survey Map shows that along the shoreline here were the remains of a submarine forest similar to that once found at Meols. The fossilized teeth of extinct animals have also been picked up here.

It was custom in the 1880s to carry children down to the water, straight from their beds, wrapped in their blankets. They were dipped three times, re-rolled in their blankets, taken back by the bathing women and put to bed again.

The Campion Family of Parkgate. From left in the back row: Jim (had no family and emigrated), Margaret (married a Middleton), Jin, (married a Taylor and emigrated), christian name not known (married a Lewis), Kate (married a Peters, and mother of J.W. Peters, greengrocers, Neston and better known as Joe, see page 53), then Jack who had no family. Front row: Mary (married Peers, and lived at the Green Cottage, Mill Street, Neston), Annie (married Metcalf), Zebbie (married Roscoe and lived at Rock Ferry). In the framed picture: John and Mary Campion (*née* Roberts) who lived at Parkgate. John came from Lincolnshire sometime in the 1800s and was a fisherman.

One of the local fishermen with a shrimping net passing the Watch House.

Transport for the female shrimpers in the early days was a faithful donkey with side panniers.
Each carried an additional basket clutched with one arm.

Jack Mealor, third from the right, with other fishermen on the Middle Strip. In 1914 he joined the Cheshire Regiment as a sniper and after the war he opened a fish shop in Parkgate. He was fishing at the age of thirteen years at Park West and died at the age of 61.

This is his son 'Enny' standing by his boat at Heswall, where it has been taken to be repaired. During the Second World War he served aboard a mine sweeper. His son Charlie still carries on the family tradition as a fisherman and the shop is still going strong.

The Middle Slip is a hive of activity as fishermen unload sacks of cockles and mussels from their boats and transfer them to their pony and carts to transport them to their homes for cleaning and sorting.

Compared to the picture above, this is a very high tide. The Middle Slip is nearly covered over so unloading takes place at the top end.

As the shore silts up fishing boats can no longer unload at the Middle Slip. Here, and in the close up view below, it can be seen how the pony and cart have become indispensable. (J. Ryan colln.)

When the mud flats became solid, with no tides floating over them, people could venture out to witness the unloading of the boats.

An advertisement card for Parkgate Convalescence Home sent to a lady in Tadcaster from her grandson Thomas in 1906. He says; 'Hope you will like my new residence. I am enjoying myself very much. we are right against the river. There is a gentle breeze blowing. Your loving grandson, Thomas. xxxx.'

Worlds apart. Workers, including a young boy with a wheelbarrow, and business men in suits carrying Gladstone bags.

On the Shore at Parkgate.

Shortly after 1900 these single-masted fishing boats with distinctive sails were seen on the Dee and were known as Parkgate 'Nobbies'.

A Stormy Day at Parkgate.

A stormy day at Parkgate in 1918. The highest tides always came with a south west wind and once or twice a year the locals reverted to the Rope Walk instead of the Promenade.

Parkgate Infant School was built in 1860 and served the needs of the young children of Parkgate for over a hundred years. These are the pupils who attended the school in 1910.

A day out in 1912. This view shows that Parkgate was once a popular place for families to take the sea air and for children to romp about in the sea.

Behind the sitters can be seen one of the wooden staircases with a hand rail that led down to the beach. There were several of these situated at intervals along the promenade.

PARK-GATE.

The stone blocks seen here are believed to have been, at one time, part of the old quay.

The promenade building with the cast-iron balcony was once known as the Assembly Room and was used, amongst other things, for public functions.

The address on this postcard reads; Bombardier Willmott, 1st Battery, 1st Worcestershire R.G.A. Volunteers Camp, Parkgate. 10th August 1903. The writer (female) asked her friend to 'be at Woodside Station at 5 p.m. to catch the 5.12 p.m. to Parkgate'.

An army unit arriving at Parkgate Station, 1907. On the back it says; 'Still alive and kicking, the other side is when we arrived on Sunday, you will see my clock in the 5th line from opposite the white gate, but nearest the railway.' (J. Ryan colln.)

The Lancashire Volunteer Artillery returning to their camp on Park Field after firing practice across the estuary from the north end of Parkgate. Photograph taken on 12 July 1903.

The nearby fields called Park Field were used by volunteer Artillery units for summer camps. This postcard was sent to Worcester 15 August 1907, (see opposite) says, 'This is a view of our Church Service held here last Sunday.'

PARKGATE PROMENADE. 100. N°36. ФВ

Prior to the 1914-18 war the sight of artillery units exercising their horses along the promenade during the summer was commonplace. This postcard was sent in 1913 to the parents of a boy at Mostyn House School, and he has marked its position with an 'X'.

A photograph of Colonel Behrend with a group of fellow officers during World War I. He lived at Malindi, Wood Lane, Parkgate.

An advertisement card for Leighton Day and Boarding School for girls. The Principals were the Misses Richardson. It was a fee paying school for the education of young ladies. It is now the Parkgate Hotel.

Notice the contrast between this view and the one below. From the Donkey Stand the sea view is one of tranquillity, with the fishing boats at anchor, whilst below is a hive of activity with the fishing fleet in full sale.

The 'Warrens', right, was the home of Harold Gill who died in 1961. He was the last professional Dee wildfowler and his exploits are still talked about over a glass of beer at the Red Lion and at the Harp.

PARKGATE.

THE PUBLIC are respectfully informed, that the ROYAL GEORGE COACH has commenced running to the above place, from the WHITE LION INN, Chester, and will continue every afternoon, except Sundays, at THREE O'CLOCK, and return from the Mostyn Arms Hotel, Parkgate, every morning, except Sunday, at NINE O'CLOCK.

It is presumed the above Conveyance will afford a convenient accommodation to Parkgate visitors, as well as to the public in general.

Performed by { M. TOMLINSON, Chester.
AND
E. BRISCOE, Parkgate.

This advertisement for a stage coach service between Chester and Parkgate appeared in the *Chester Courant* at the beginning of the nineteenth century. After her husband's death, Mrs Esther Briscoe refurbished the old inn and in 1819 renamed it the Mostyn Hotel.

This photograph taken in the 1880s shows the old front of Mostyn House School. It had been refurbished in 1818 from the George Inn.

The opening of Mostyn house School chapel in 1897. The chapel's foundation stone was laid 14 October 1895 by J.M. Wilson, Archdeacon of Manchester and formerly Headmaster of Clifton, when A.G. Grenfell was a boy there. The opening ceremony, a service of dedication, was performed by the Bishop of Chester 4 November 1897. The date was picked because 4 November was A.G.'s birthday. We see here the procession of staff and clergy as they walked towards the chapel for the service of dedication. A.G. Grenfell is the bald-headed man with the glasses at the rear of the staff and his brother Wilfred is behind him. The Bishop is at the end of the procession.

MOSTYN HOUSE SCHOOL, FROM BASE OF QUAY WALL.

This is the west side of the school in 1904. It received its black and white mock-tudor face-lift in 1932 when the older buildings, to the left, were in danger of collapse.

As in most public schools of the period, learning to handle firearms was considered an essential part of the development of a young boy. Here Mostyn House boys are practicing with carbines on the sands at the base of the Quay wall 4 July 1903.

Sir Wilfred Grenfell was born 28 February 1865 in Mostyn House. His boyhood was spent among the marshes and saltings of the Dee. He qualified as a doctor in London and left for Labrador in 1892 where he spent the next forty years of his life. He was knighted in 1927 and died in 1940.

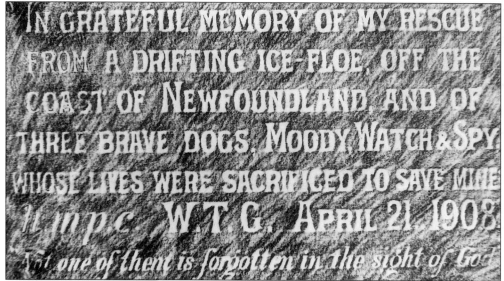

IN GRATEFUL MEMORY OF MY RESCUE FROM A DRIFTING ICE-FLOE, OFF THE COAST OF NEWFOUNDLAND, AND OF THREE BRAVE DOGS, MOODY, WATCH & SPY WHOSE LIVES WERE SACRIFICED TO SAVE MINE
R.I.P.C. W.T.G. APRIL 21, 1908
Not one of them is forgotten in the sight of God

A rubbing of a brass plate in the chapel of Mostyn House. Another version is in St Anthony's Hospital, Newfoundland. This commemorates the incident, in which Wilfred Grenfell killed and skinned three members of his dogsled team and used their coats as a shelter, to save his life.

A portrait of Algernon Grenfell who became Headmaster of Mostyn House in 1890. He is seen sitting with his dog Rag and his brother Wilfred in Mostyn House in 1932.

This is an eight foot tall statue of Sir Wilfred Grenfell which stands in front of the Confederation Building in St John's, Newfoundland. It was made by Hans Melling and was unveiled in 1970.

The staff at Mostyn House in 1936. It includes A.G. Grenfell MA, headmaster, (behind the alsation dog), Matron and the games coach (right).

A class in progress in the 1930s.

When the tide is out the flat sandbanks make it ideal for boys to learn the rudiments of sailing with the aid of sand yachts, 1930s.

Under the supervision of an ex-Chief Petty Officer RN the boys then went to the real thing, sailing '12 Footers'. Here with a fair breeze and the safety of a life jacket, the boys are sailing the shallow waters of the Dee estuary.

George Ward Gunn was born in 1912 and came to Mostyn House School in 1923. His three brothers followed him and their father was the school doctor. This photograph was taken six months before he left the school. He became a Second Lieutenant in the 3rd Regiment, Royal Artillery in 1940. On 21 November 1941 at Sidi Rezegh, Libya, an attack by thirty German tanks was countered by four anti-tank guns under the command of Second Lieutenant Gunn. During the engagement this officer drove from gun to gun in an unarmoured vehicle and when three of his guns were destroyed and the crew of the fourth either dead or disabled, he took charge of the remaining gun. He managed to fire fifty rounds and set two enemy tanks on fire before he himself was killed. He was gazetted the Victoria Cross 21 April 1942, having already received the Military Cross.

A two coach, diesel multiple unit at Parkgate Station 21 April 1961. The crew were on a training run.

The sandbanks have long gone and this scene in the 1950s is not much different from today, as we head off for Gayton and beyond.

Four

Heswall

This toll-house guarded the old Chester High Road, as did the one at Woodbank. The gentleman with the cycle was Thomas Parry a native of Liverpool, a keen cyclist and photographer, 1922.

The Chester High Road with the Toll Bar Cottage in the distance. Toll bars once had a circle of pike heads in them to deter horse riders from jumping over them to avoid paying the toll. The name 'turnpike' for these roads is believed to have originated from this.

The Mersey Railway started a Sunday bus service to the Glegg Arms (above) from Central Station on Boxing Day 1905. On 14 January 1905 it was extended into Heswall to the Mount corner with Telegraph Road. The journey took fifty minutes, and the fares were 1/- single, 1/6d return. The service ceased after Birkenhead Corporation objected and, after litigation, won their case.

Gayton, or Heswall, mill was reputed to be the oldest tower windmill in Wirral. In the sixteenth century it belonged to the Glegg family of Gayton Hall. There are several eighteenth-century documents dealing with the windmill and lands both here and in other parts of Wirral involving William Glegg and Sarah Rigby of Liverpool dated 24 May 1766. In the small antiquated cottage next to the mill, (bottom picture) the last miller brought up a family of sixteen children. In 1850, Samuel and James Woodward were the millers.

This ship the *Thomas* was a loaded collier from the Ness Colliery that was wrecked about 1880.
In 1907 it was in the middle of a big bank, a long way from the 'deep'. When this picture was
taken on February 1913, it was on the edge of a 'deep' and local fishermen could board it for free
coal.

This is the Causey Wall end opposite Flint, with its beacon which was lit by electric light for the first time 15 December 1913.

'A Fowler in the position for Flighting in frozen ice floes of the Dee estuary in the 1890s. In hard weather some excellent shooting can be had among the ice, if you sit down within range of any of the many springs of fresh water that run down from the shore. Completely hidden by the ice the birds cannot see you till well within range. It's advisable to keep the gun cocked.'

Gayton Cottage in 1908 when it was occupied by L.N. Brookes, a wildfowler. Once known as Gayton Boat House, it was for a long time the property, and occasionally the residence, of the Glegg family of Gayton Hall. The vestry meeting for the parish churchwardens was held here at Easter in 1819.

L.N. Brookes and his second wife, pose with their dogs not far from their home at Gayton Cottage.

Leonard Brookes, seen here on the right, originally operated his gun punt around Burton, but because of the channels silting up he moved, in 1890, to Gayton. He is seen here with his puntsman, Tom Evans, a local fisherman of Heswall.

This group was known as the 'Clan Evans' gathering around the gun punt in January 1907. From the left: Dick, Jack, Tom, young Dick (Kruger) and Sam. Young Dick fell overboard and was drowned in Dawpool 30 July 1907.

Out in the estuary before heading for a likely target area.

Searching for a target. There is a seven yard recoil on a punt gun, so you need that much space behind you before you fire the gun.

Leonard Brookes (right) in his punt, with fisherman Tom Evans at the end of a successful shoot.

Leonard Brookes striding ashore with some of the days shoot. His home, Gayton Cottage, is in the background.

Although much of this building has been altered and extended it was once Gayton Ferry House. It is marked as such on Greenwood's 1819 map of Cheshire and operated to Greenfield in Flintshire. A ferry is on record as having being used in 1277 by Edward I who crossed over from Gayton to Flint after a stay at Shotwick Castle.

The shoreline at Heswall in 1909.

The shore at Heswall where a pony and trap awaits the return of the fishermen with their day's catch of fish and shell fish.

98

THE SHORE, HESWALL. 211224

At the end of a week of bombing in May 1941 the shoreline here was littered with shrapnel and unexploded incendiary bombs.

Beach Approach, Heswall. FRITH HWL 6

Heswall Sailing Club began in January 1919. Their original flag was a salmon on a red background and remained so for forty years after which it changed to a leaping salmon. The first clubhouse was situated at the bottom of Bank Road.

Heswall, The Shore

Down below the Railway Station there used to be a row of terraced houses called Flukebone Cottages which were occupied mostly by fishermen whose boats were anchored off Heswall shore. Mostyn Avenue, down by the shore, is where most of the fishermen now live.

Elizabeth (Cissie) Smith (see page 35) a miner's daughter from Ness at seventeen years, when she became engaged to Henry Evans, twenty one years, a fisherman from Heswall. They were married in Neston 24 June 1936. They had eight children, four boys and four girls and were married for thirty nine years. She still lives in Mostyn Avenue surrounded by her own 'Clan Evans'.

West Park which terminates at Marine Parade in the scene opposite *c.* 1912. (J. Ryan colln.)

Gayton Wakes were held every Michaelmas, until the First World War, in the fields opposite the hotel. People would travel over from Flint on the ferry boat to Gayton Ferry house to attend.

This photograph was taken after the Post Office had moved from the building next door on the left. (Pub. J. Geo. Davies, Port Sunlight)

Outside Heswall Post Office a group of young postmen pose for the photographer.

Between the thatched cottage and the slate-roofed that juts out, was the entrance to one of three smithies in the area. In the slate-roofed cottages lived a family of fishermen called the Prices. Their youngest son Bob was lost off Hilbre Island in a storm.

A. Youds confectionery later became Atherton's cake shop. A former resident remembers, as a young boy, delivering bread and cakes around Heswall on Saturday afternoons for half-crown.

The bottom of the 'Wallrake' leading up to Dawstone Road in 1912. The definition of 'Wallrake' is, a lane at, or to, a well.

BROW LANE, HESWALL.

"The Unions Series"

Brow Lane was the old name for School Lane, changed because of the school built there (see page 106). School sports were held in the grounds of Ruscote which belonged to the Brocklebank family. The boundary wall of Roscote can be seen in the top picture on page 103.

Rock Lane was originally known as Pinnacle Road, a name still inscribed on a sandstone wall on the left of the lane, leaving the village. It has also been known as Hillhouse Road.

The once peaceful road to Thurstaston. Elder Cottage was the original village school until 1872.

Looking up School Hill to the school buildings on the left. The seat shown in the Brow Hill picture on the previous page is to the right of the lady cyclist. (J. Ryan colln.)

SCHOOL HILL, HESWALL.

P & Co LD

During May 1941, Heswall was bombed for a week. St Peter's school lost three classrooms. The headmaster's daughter and her fiancee were killed.

The year is 1906 and this is the bottom of School Hill and the old Black Horse which later became the Heswall Hotel.

✳

This advertisement card was sent from the Heswall Hotel to Portugal 17 December 1909 and arrived there 21 December 1909. How it got back here again, goodness only knows! (J. Ryan colln.)

Heswall Football Club, 1911. Back row: Mr Green (Chairman), G. Law, A. Wilson, N. Brain, A. Stone, A. Woods, -?-, T. Power, -?-, S. Tudor, W. Williams, T. Briscoe, S. Edge. Front row: A. Atwell, J. Buckley, J. Williams, R. Price, -?-.

Heswall Football Club 1920. Back row: B. Edge, S. Edge, A. Woods, T. Briscoe, J. Dodd. Middle row: A. Wilson, B. Edwards, D. Hughes, A. Hughes, E. Swift, T. Peers. Front row: F. Law, -?-, A. Stone, J. Sillitcoe, D. Price.

On Sunday, 19 September 1875 there was a terrific thunderstorm, accompanied by torrents of rain, during the evening service. Lightning struck the weather vane on the flagpole of the tower and passed through the building into the gallery and the body of the church below and two men were killed: a young schoolmaster from Neston, John Heveran, deputising for the usual organist, and Henry Rathbone, a young Heswall farm servant. Several others were injured and considerable damage was done to the building. The storm caused houses in Parkgate to be flooded and the bridge at Barnston to collapse.

This photograph shows restoration of the tower of St Peter's Church.

David Griffiths, one time Sexton of St Peter's.

The man in the white shirt is David Griffiths who was born in 1872 and married Mary Walker. They had one child named Mary Elizabeth, and first lived in Birkenhead, then moved to Heswall. As a young man he walked to work in Birkenhead and helped to build the fire station. He was later sexton of St Peter's Church.

Mary Elizabeth Griffiths at her home, Wellwood Cottage, in Lower Heswall. In the background is Elder Cottage (see page 105) and around the corner is the Black Horse Inn (Heswall Hotel).

This is Mary Elizabeth on her wedding day. She married Joseph Ashton from Willaston in 1920 and the wedding group was taken outside Wellwood Cottage which was to become their home. They had one son and a daughter born here; David in 1922 and Winifred in 1925.

David Ashton (centre) with two of his cousins outside Wellwood Cottage in about 1930.

Two views of Lower Heswall Station. In this one, taken in 1905, the signalman is approaching the incoming train waith a 'staff' to give to the engine driver, showing there was no train on the single line section he was about to enter, onwards to Thurstaston.

The station in 1917. This station was opened in 1886 and was the only rail-link until Heswall Hills Station was opened 1 May 1898 on the Bidston to North Wales branch line. (J. Ryan colln.)

The bottom end of the Lydiate coming off Rectory Lane and winding up to the lower village.

Lydiate House, to the left of the tree, was converted into a shop by a family called Shones. The Lydiate had some of the earliest gas lamps in the area, leading the way to the railway station.

The War Memorial, Heswall.

Mr C. Thompson reading the names on the Roll of Honour at the First Armistice Day Service at Heswall War Memorial on the corner of Mount Road and Dee View Road. The Akbar School Boys' Band played hymns.

According to Slater's *Trade Directory* for 1869 there were smithies at Heswall, Joseph Smallwood, and at Gayton, Obadiah Cunningham and Thomas Barlow. At this smithy in Dawstone Road the last blacksmith is reputed to have been a Barlow.

In 1912 Dawstone Road held a number of large houses in their own grounds. A local lady who had been 'in service' in one of them said the household servants were; a nanny, an under-nanny, a housemaid, a parlourmaid and a between-maid. The outside staff consisted of a chauffeur, two gardeners and an under-gardener.

This is the iron ore train passing through Heswall Hills Station on its way to John Summers & Sons Ltd., Hawarden Bridge Steel Works, at Shotton. Because of the steep gradients the iron ore hopper trains required large locomotives to pull them.

The Bidston to North Wales line was occasionally used for other traffic. This is a day excursion train from Birmingham to New Brighton passing Heswall Hills signal box.

The Church Lads Brigade in 1901 on the lawn of the old Rectory.

The Church Lads Brigade, Heswall, Coy. No.19, sometime in the 1920s.

These two pictures show the changing scene in Pensby Road from 1907 to 1913, respectively.

This scene from 1909, looks back at the crossroads with Telegraph Road and, straight ahead, to The Mount. (J. Ryan colln.)

Straight across here and you are heading for Thurstaston, to the right, Pensby Road, and to the left, The Mount.

This was the grocery shop of John Irwin & Company in Heswall. Seen here in the 1930s, it shows the staff outside the shop and the delivery van with its driver.

This is The Mount before the First World War. This postcard was sold and published by local photographer H. Middleton Jones of Heswall.

Telegraph Road crossroads in 1911, quite different from today! Straight across for the Glegg Arms, to the left, Pensby Road, to the right, The Mount and the lower village.

It is said that Telegraph Road is named after a nineteenth-century telegraph station that was on top of Heswall Hill. If this is so, it was not part of the Holyhead to Liverpool 1827-58 telegraph system which was only used for shipping.

An outing for Heswall Silver Band. An old Barnston resident, Les Jones, recalls Jack Pye's bus service was called 'The Old Silver Queen'. When the midnight bus for Heswall left Prenton terminus there would be passengers hanging on the running boards.

John 'Jack' Pye is believed to have started his bus service in about 1916. The route to Birkenhead was via Pensby and the buses had terminated at the corner of Singleton Avenue and Borough Road and connected with the trams on the Prenton route. After the war more routes were added, to Thurstaston and Irby and in 1921 a route to Barnston. Later still a service was started between Parkgate and Prenton Tram Terminus via Thornton Hough and Clatterbridge. The ground floor of the present Gateway Stores in Telegraph Road was used as a garage and a bus station and a waiting room were built to shelter passengers. Local people remember his habit of calling for you if you overslept! He had a rival in Johnson's of Birkenhead, and locals talk about the mad races between the two companies. Eventually the company was bought out in January 1924 by the Crosvile Traction Company of Chester.

In addition to the Heswall service Jack Pye started a coach service from Rhos-on-Sea from about 1922. After his business in Heswall was taken over he went to Colwyn Bay and built a business up there. The man in the centre, with the trilby, is either 'Johnny' or one of his sons at the Colwyn Bay Garage. The business was run by the family until 1965.

Heswall Bus Station is believed to be the first bus station to have been built in this country. This is a view of the garage for buses at the old Crosvile Bus Station in Heswall in 1947.

Outside the bus station in Telegraph Road are a bus driver and conductor awaiting a changeover. Further down on the right can be seen the King's Cinema.

Through trains could still be seen travelling on the Hooton to West Kirby branch line but the last passenger train left West Kirby 15 September 1956. The Royal Train travelled on this line 11 July 1957. There were also special trains bringing service personnel to the Royal Air Force camp at West Kirby. Cadbury's used special trains for trade delegations visiting their new factory at Moreton and trains for taking their employees to various places. The two trains illustrated here were for Cadbury's employees en route to Evesham, passing through Hooton Station 22 June 1961.

The original building which formed the Cleaver Sanatorium in the early 1920s. Later on, three-storied extensions were added to either side of the above building.

Both the Cleaver Sanatorium and the Royal Liverpool Children's Hospital were built on the slopes of the hills facing the Dee estuary to take advantage of the prevailing winds that blew in from the sea bringing fresh air!.

CHILDREN'S HOSPITAL, HESWALL.

This magnificent building took four years to build, from 1905 until 1909. The picture below shows the open air extensions at the back. Sadly all this is now gone to be replaced by a Tesco Superstore.

Open-air Wards Children's Hospital, Heswall.

Open air wards with glass sliding partitions were widely used in the 1920s and 30s in T.B. wards, because it was widely believed that fresh air would help to clear congested lungs.

The *Akbar* was the first training ship to be moored in the River Mersey, it came in 1856. The other three were; the *Conway* 1859, the *Indefatigable* 1864 and the *Clarence* in 1864. The ship in the middle is the *Akbar*.

The *Akbar* became a shore establishment at Heswall in 1907. There was a ship in the grounds constructed of concrete and used for training purposes. At the Church of England School Sports Day, the boys from the *Akbar* gave gymnastic displays and their band provided music.

HESWALL CAMP AND CLUB, LIVERPOOL BOYS ASSOCIATION   L 2915

Liverpool, like many other cities from the 1920s, onwards established camping sites in rural areas that were adjacent to the sea for young boys of deprived or poor families to benefit from a change of surroundings and fresh air. In the bottom view, a message on the back says; 'Arrow shows the bungalows, we had no tents, The house is the caretaker's premises.'

L.B.A. CAMP DEESIDE, HESWALL.

A diesel unit (see page 86) on a training run at Heswall Station.

On 26 May 1962 the last freight train serving the station on the Hooton to West Kirby line arrived at Hooton Station. The driver is seen here passing the 'staff' for the last time. The locomotive was a Stainer Fairburn 4MT Class 264 Tank Engine, No. 42229.

The demolition train is seen here in 1963 in Heswall Station on its way to the station sidings.

From Heswall stationyard sidings the demolition train went out each day to remove track and lineside signalling equipment from the area.

Apart from a short period (see page 99) Heswall escaped the brunt of the German air raids on Merseyside. Here are some of those that took part in the war effort from Horburys Munitions Factory, in Pye Road, Heswall c. 1940. At the very back is Stella Mari Gaskin, and amongst the rest can be found: Mrs Davis, Edie Gaskell, Mrs Shakeshaft, Jim Williams, Olive Scott, Mable Williams, Kath Pumford, Miss Thompson, Mrs Watt. Front row: Griffiths, Rita Doyle, Alice Powell, Mrs Rutter.

Five
Around Heswall

Behind the group of children in Barnston village can be seen the large window of the village store and Post Office, In 1906 John Jones was sub-postmaster and in 1923 Thomas Johns is described as the grocer and assistant overseer at the Post Office.

BARNSTON VILLAGE.   "The Unique Series".

The same background was visible on the previous page but because the trees have no leaves on them, you can see the buildings. First, Bank Farm then, in between, Storeton Lane, then Bank House and furthest away, Beech Farm.

Barnston Church of England School in 1908. The schoolmaster was Mr Barker. The boy second from the left in the back row, is Sid Evans.

134

Barnston Church of England School, performing Mayday festivities before the First World War. From the left: George Francom, second girl from the left, between the two boys, Mona Newby. The boy, furthest right is Willy Morrison.

Barnston Church of England School May Queen. At the back, the guide on the left is C. Buchanan and on the right, B. Morrision. Back row: E. Shakeshaft, E. Trueman, J. Benson, P. Newby. Next row: I. Newby, M. Prance, R. Roberts May Queen, A. Okell, J. Prance. Front row: E. Jones, A. Roberts, B. Smith, -?-.

Barnston Church of England School, Empire Day. The May Queen was Nancy Newby who was born in 1904 and died aged 90 years. She lived in Barnston all of her life and her son, Frank Prince, still lives in Pensby. Her daughter Molly is in Ipswich. Nancy was one of five girls, and four of her sisters are alive today.

Barnston Church of England School. Back row: T. Kendrick, W. Gardener, P. Williams, W. Morris, B. Oxton, G. Francom, F. Gardener, J. Leesing (Storeton House Farm). Middle row: M.E. Jones, -?-, -?-, N. Barker, M. Bennett, E. Trueman, Walter Langley Roberts (Headmaster). Front row: N. Benson, P. Newby, M. Newby, J. Prance, L. Shakeshaft, B. Smith, A. Roberts.

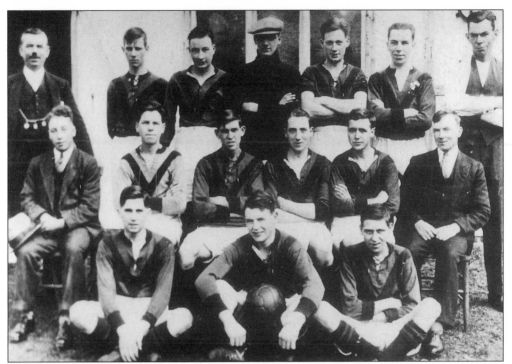

Barnston Football Team, 1930-31. Some of the team were as follows: Nobby Williams, his son Ronnie Frank Sherlock (Manor Farm), Ben Francis of Holmewood Avenue, Harold Williams, John Jack Price, (his parents were landlords of the Fox and Hounds), Fred Braden Brerton, Leslie Jones, Jack Jones, Jimmy Morrision and Jack Gardiner.

This is an early view of Storeton Station which was the nearest place for people travelling to Dale Farm Picnic Grounds. At weekends and holiday periods people travelled from afar to enjoy the various amusements.

The building with the wheel propped against the wall was the local wheelwright in Barnston Dale.

This charming view shows the yard at the rear of the wheelwright's premises.

Many years ago 'Old Polly Gertrey' used to whitewash the sandstone steps of the Fox and Hounds every morning. She also polished the counter down with paraffin wax and made the place stink of paraffin!

In the last century the license holder was required to have a team of horses to assist travellers up the hill out of Barnston Dale. An old custom of tracing patterns on the floor by using fresh dock leaves was continued until 1910.

The boy sitting on the steps, talking to the young girl, was Les Jones, The old inn was demolished in 1910 and a new one built. From 1944 until 1946 the landlord was Joseph Millington. His son Leslie took over and ran it until 1968.

The Fox and Hounds clad with festive bunting for the Queens Coronation, June 1953. Standing outside, from left to right are: Elsie Boulter, Irene Millington, Joseph Millington, his son Leslie and Theresa Millington.

In the days before the First World War, Scott's Farm or Dale House Farm Picnic Grounds, were the most popular place in the area.

Liverpool people came by train to Storeton Station, whereas Birkenhead people came in flat waggons, with benches for passengers, drawn by horse teams from the Oxton Carriage & Waggon Company.

There were fairground amusements as well as sports grounds. The picnic grounds were situated in Storeton Lane about half-a-mile from Barnston village and in fifteen acres of Barnston Dale.

Since 1989 Barnston Dale camp has been run by a private trust for local youth associations, with dormitories, a sporting complex and areas for outdoor activities.

142

This is an example of one of the many postcards that visitors could purchase at the shop in the picnic grounds as a souvenir of their visit.

This is Bank Farm where horse and waggons were kept, to convey people to and from the railway station. The farm is still survives at the corner of Storeton Lane and Barnston Road.

This is Jim Jones' corner shop at the corner of Gills Lane and Pensby Road in the early 1900s.

Pensby Cubs, 1952-53. Back row: John Sherlock, -?-, -?-, James McAllister, -?-. Front row: -?-, Colin Deakins, Dave Catheral, Peter Duckers.

Thingwall Mill was a large brick edifice with a walking stage around it in 1866, and succeeded an earlier one without a stage. A well-known family of millers by the name of Capper worked this mill for nearly two centuries. It was well-known for its oatmeal, a considerable amount of which was sent to Liverpool. The arms of the old mill came within a few inches of the ground and several pigs and other animals are known to have been killed by the revolving arms. On New Years Day, 1897, one of the arms was blown down and shortly afterwards Robert Capper died. Since then it ceased to operate. On Mrs Capper's death in 1900, the mill was bought for £50 by a local farmer, who resold it to a Liverpool timber merchant for twice the sum and it was then demolished.

In the early 1900s the detached shop on the left was H. Rowe's, grocer and saddler. The landlady of the Coach and Horses in the background at that time was Mrs Margaret Rose.

The shop next to the Coach and Horses belonged to Mrs E. Disbury and the blacksmith next door was William Disbury. The back of this postcard has a printed Christmas scene with festive greetings and was sent by W. and E.H. Hockenhull.

Elm Stores in 1925 was managed by B. Clarke. The local boy scouts look to be in danger of being knocked down by the cyclists.

This view of Irby Post Office was taken in 1921. The sub postmaster in 1923 was Edward Roland Jones.

The open spaces around Irby Hill have always been popular for picnics and day outings. In 1911 this group of people were out on their annual picnic and pose for a photographic postcard souvenir of the event. (J. Ryan colln.)

Corner House Farm. A local railwayman pauses to be included in a photograph for posterity. Could this be the same group of scouts that were outside the Elm Stores?

Irby Mill was the last remaining peg mill in Wirral. An earlier mill stood well up the hill to the south of this one and was destroyed in 1773.

This was the second mill built by Richard Hale in 1776, which stopped working in 1888. In 1898 three men offered to pull the ruined mill down. Instead of inserting timber and firing it, they knocked out the brickwork and ran! Thomas Parry was miller in 1868-9 and William Atkinson in 1883.

Frank Lester was born in Huyton, Liverpool 18 February 1896, the son of John and Ellen Lester. His parents moved to Wirral when he was a young boy and settled in Irby, at Mill Hill Road. At the outbreak of war he became a private in the 10th Bn. Lancashire Fusiliers and was killed 12 October 1918. An extract from the *London Gazette* December 13 1918 records, 'During the clearing of the village of Neuvilly, Pte. Lester observed that an enemy sniper was causing heavy casualties to a party across the street. Dashing out to deal with him, he fell mortally wounded. To save their lives he sacrificed his own'. He was awarded the Victoria Cross.

The local road sweeper passing Bennett's Cottage on Mill Hill Road. (J. Ryan colln.)

Irby Mill Road, at the junction with Manor Road, looking towards Irby village. (J. Ryan colln.)

On Thurstaston Hill looking out over the Dee estuary with the hills of Wales in the distance.

Thurstaston Camp in 1938. Lord Lever at Port Sunlight works started up a compulsory Holiday Club by deducting one hour's pay from the employee's wages on which the company paid four per cent interest. In 1919 he was able to acquire a site nine miles from the factory at Thurstaston for a week-end camp. Sexes were segregated at first, but later family huts were built. Rent was 10/- per week.

A group of agricultural workers on a local farm at harvest time at the turn of the century.

Dressed with HADFIELD'S
LIVERPOOL PREPARED BONE COMPOUND
BY MESSRS W & J HOUGH.
THURSTASTON. CHESHIRE

This was an advertisement postcard issued by Hadfields of Liverpool who manufactured prepared bone compound as a fertiliser used by W. & J. Hough, Thurstaston. The card is dated 1907 and William Hough still farmed Thurstaston Hall in 1923. (J. Ryan colln.)

Thurstaston Hall was with the Whitmore family from the fourteenth century until the beginning of this. Part of the buildings may be as old as the fifteenth century. The west wing dates from 1680, and the front from about 1700.

The house has a ghost which was sketched by an artist staying there. Sometime later the artist was visiting a family in the south of England and recognised one of the family portraits as being identical to the sketch. It transpired that their ancestors had once lived at Thurstaston Hall!

This is the Parish School of St Bartholomews, Thurstaston, also called Dawpool School. It was built in 1859 by the late Joseph Hegan and the pupils included children from Irby.

Tidying up the road outside the school. Both photographs are from 'The Wirral Series' by local photographer E.R. Jones.

The houses in the background were railwaymen's cottages adjacent to the station below. The old gentleman appears to be wearing a uniform. The postcard is dated 1907 and the writer says he lives in one of the houses in the pictures.

This is a view of Thurstaston station in the early 1900s. The station was some distance from the village. The engine appears to be a Great Western Railway Tank Engine and the number on the side is No. 1401.

A Red Letter Day for the Hooton to West Kirby branch line came nine months after it closed its passenger service. On Thursday afternoon 11 July 1957 the Royal Train with the Queen on board used the branch line on its way to West Kirby. The line was fully checked for safety by the length gangs and everywhere was spruced up. This view shows the two 2-6-4 tank engines hauling the Royal Train past the goods siding at Thurstaston. The four lamps on the front of the foremost engine indicate, to railwaymen, its status. The train crews from Hooton Station to West Kirby were: G. Roberts (driver, from Hoole Lane, Chester), J.D. Evans (fireman, from Bridgemond Road, Chester), W.L. Roberts (driver, from Audrene, Maytree Avenue, Chester), J.A. Jackson (fireman, from Paradise Row, Chester), W. Owen (guard, from Vernon Road, Chester).

This is the demolition train based in Heswall sidings taking up the track in Thurstaston in 1963.

The job is completed at Thurstaston station, marking the end of an era.

Looking down from Thurstaston Cliff onto Dawpool. The name was derived from a lost hamlet recorded here in 1454.

In this isolated spot, down by the shoreline, once lived an old lady called Sally McCrae. She lived here alone, all her life, and died in her eighties, about forty years ago.

Acknowledgemnts

A book such as this can only be achieved by the generosity and help of many people who have gone out of their way and lent me family photographs, postcards and shared their memories and local knowlegde to bring the pictures to life.

I would like to thank the following people; Mr D. Ashton, Mr I. Boumphrey, Mr S. Buckley, Mr Stuart and Mrs Polly Carter, Mrs A.E. Congreve, Mr R. Craven, Mrs E. Evans (Cissie) and family, Mr R. Hignett, Mr Ted Gerry, Mrs G. Jackson, Mr Monty Lister (Radio Merseyside), Mr and Mrs C. Mealor, Mr C. Millington, Mr Paul Mitchell, Mr G. Pearson, Mr G. Place, Mr L. Smith, Mr T. Turner. Mr E. Wakelam, President of Heswall Football Club, Mr Teg Williams, Mr Wilf Wilson.

A very special thanks to the following: Mr Julian Grenfell MA (Cantab) Headmaster of Mostyn House School, Mike Lister industrial history author, Mr T.B. Maund transport historian and author, Mr Bill Norton Principal Librarian of Bibliographical and Computer Services, Wirral Libraries, Mr Glyn Parry for his expertise in copying old photographs, Mr John Ryan who helped in many ways, The Bromborough Society, The Burton Historical Society, The Parkgate Society, The Williamson Art Gallery, Mr P.F. Mason Assistant Archivist Clwyd Record Office, Mrs P. James, Curator of the Queens Royal Surrey Regiment Museum, R.D. Cassidy MBE Major (Retd), Curator The Royal Green Jackets Museum, J. McHallam Major (Retd) Curator The Royal Regiment Of Fusilers Museum, The Reference Library Staff of Chester City, Ellesmere Port, Heswall, Irby and Neston Libraries, Mary Carol, Barbara, Debbie of Max Spielman's for their invaluable help.

I dedicate this book to my wife,
Norah Rowena,
in this our Golden Wedding Year.